"Tony's style and substance have never been better! In a gripping way, he leads us beyond the ordinary toward the potential, limitless work of God in our lives. Read this, and take it personally."

DR. JOSEPH STOWELL

"For the many difficult and seemingly unanswerable conditions that people face in life today, Dr. Tony Evans in his inimitable way of exceptional exposition and insightful wisdom illustrates for us how God weaves His will and His truth through our human situations in order to accomplish His ultimate purposes in our lives."

DR. E. K. BAILEY, SENIOR PASTOR OF CONCORD MISSIONARY BAPTIST CHURCH, DALLAS, TEXAS

"Tony Evans is one of the great preachers in America today. When he speaks or writes, I listen—and recommend that others do so as well!"

CHUCK COLSON

"God has given Dr. Tony Evans a unique ability to talk straight about truth. With fewer words than perhaps anyone I know, he can get to the heart of a matter and put it into biblical perspective. *God Is Up to Something Great* will thrill you with its message about our wise and sovereign Heavenly Father's plan for your life. Especially if you think your past precludes a positive future, read it. It will encourage and help you to experience more of the wonder of God's love."

FRANKLIN GRAHAM, PRESIDENT AND CEO, SAMARITAN'S PURSE
AND BILLY GRAHAM EVANGELISTIC ASSOCIATION

GOD
Is Up to
SOMETHING GREAT

LIFECHANGE BOOKS

TONY
EVANS

Multnomah®Publishers *Sisters, Oregon*

GOD IS UP TO SOMETHING GREAT
published by Multnomah Publishers, Inc.

© 2002 by Tony Evans

International Standard Book Number: 1-59052-038-6

Cover design by Kirk DouPonce UDG/DesignWorks
Cover image by Photonica

For information:
MULTNOMAH PUBLISHERS, INC.•POST OFFICE BOX 1720
SISTERS, OREGON 97759

Library of Congress Cataloging-in-Publication Data
Evans, Anthony T.
   God is up to something great / by Tony Evans.
      p. cm.
   ISBN 1-59052-038-6 (HDPC)
   1. Christian life--Biblical teaching. 2. Paul, the Apostle, Saint. 3. Peter, the
Apostle, Saint. 4. Joseph (Son of Jacob) I. Title.
   BS680.C47 E93 2002
   248.4--dc21   2002009093

02 03 04 05 06 07 08—10 9 8 7 6 5 4 3 2 1 0

Dedication

This book is dedicated to that special person
who needs the days ahead to be better
than the days gone by.

CONTENTS

Chapter 1

THE GOOD, THE BAD, AND THE UGLY

A FEW YEARS AGO, the Soviet submarine *Kursk* went down in the Barents Sea. When diving crews reached the sunken submarine, they heard tapped SOS signals coming from inside the sub. The crew was wondering, Is there any hope?

Like those sailors, many people today feel trapped in

impossible situations. They feel like banging against their circumstances and wondering the same thing: Is there any hope?

Do you ever feel that way, wondering how your circumstances could possibly be worked out, how your life could come to mean something?

Well, let me tell you what I know is true: *God is up to something great.*

It's true. He's up to something great in every person's life. Do you believe that? Do you feel that God is up to something great in *your* life? That His plans and purposes for you are about more than just trudging through the days, wondering to yourself, *Is there really any hope? Do I have a purpose?*

This book is for people who feel that they are fresh out of hope. It's for people who've made big mistakes, who've seen every ray of sunshine turn into clouds of rain. It's for people with broken dreams and lingering disappointments—people whose hope and sense of purpose, *despite* their best efforts, have been dashed to the ground. It's even for people who've known success but still have holes in their hearts.

And not all hope-deprived people are poor either. If you have money, maybe you're spending it on psychologists, trying to find hope within yourself. Trying by mental manipulation and self-analysis to drive out anger, fear, and negativity, as though by emptying yourself of bad you might automatically be filled with good.

But hope is not the absence of despair. It's the presence of something far greater, something only God can give. Hope is not passive; it's the most active force in the world because it is derived from the most powerful Being of all: Hope comes from God. It's real. And it's never more than a moment away. And with hope comes purpose. That's the message of this book—through all the circumstances in your life, God is up to something great.

So let's get started...

I doubt Clint Eastwood ever realized that a character he played would introduce a phrase into the English language that would still be used decades later. But he did so just the same, through a movie he was in in the 1960s. I didn't see *The Good, the Bad, and the Ugly* when it first hit the silver screen, but I saw it on video years later. By that time the title had given our culture an expression that hasn't gone away for nearly forty years now.

Well, the title of the movie made me think of a guy

I knew who'd just graduated from medical school. He had been given a full scholarship, which paid all his bills and let him study twenty-four hours a day. By my reckoning, that was "good" because it was something positive and beneficial that moved him forward in life.

I knew another guy who'd been given a full scholarship to a different kind of school, to study engineering. But instead of studying and learning, he spent his time drinking beer and goofing off. He flunked out. That was "bad" because he brought disaster on himself.

I knew a third fellow who'd planned to be a surgeon. But one day a lawn mower he was using blew up and burned his hands so badly that he lost several fingers. And that was "ugly" because his dream died through something that wasn't his fault.

My question is this: How often have *you* used the terms *good, bad,* and *ugly* to characterize what's happened in your life? *All* of us go through good, bad, and just plain ugly times at one point or another.

But, friend, that's only half the story—because God is up to something great through all of it.

Through His magnificent grace, God can take the good, the bad, and the ugly experiences in your life and use them to make you unbelievably better at what He's created you for, whatever that might be! And that's what is so amazing about God—He can take *all* those good, bad, and ugly experiences and use them for your calling. That's good news, right?

In God's economy, all is redeemed and nothing is ever lost. He can take the good things that we remember most fondly, the bad things we might like to forget, and the ugly things that have shaped us into people we didn't start out to be and use *all of them* to facilitate His individual purpose for each and every one of us.

Including you.

As Job said of God: "I know that You can do all things, and that no purpose of Yours can be thwarted" (42:2). God is able to take and make whatever He wills. He can *take* whatever and whoever you are and *make* you into whatever and whoever you need to be to become your *best possible self.*

This is one of the most glorious promises in all of Christianity. If God couldn't mold us and break us—if He couldn't pull us back from the jaws of hell and turn lives of waste into lives of witness—an awful lot of us would have suffocated, drowned, or blown ourselves up a long time ago. If He couldn't take our strengths and our weaknesses and our mistakes and the bad things that have happened to us and use them for His purposes and our benefit....

Well, that's what this book is all about.

Because God *can* take the good times, the bad times, and the ugly times we all endure and use them to instruct, strengthen, and refine us for His holy purposes.

He can!

Chapter 2

WHERE NOTHING
IS EVER WASTED

WHEN I WAS IN SEMINARY, I took a job at a bus station working the night shift.

Before I'd been there very long, I realized that some of the guys I worked with were running a clever little con game almost every night. An hour after one of the players in this game had punched out, someone else would punch him back in, even though he'd already gone home. These guys had worked out a routine for rotating who was being "covered" so they could all pump up their pay-checks.

They tried to get me involved too. But I was a Christian, and I said it was wrong. And because I said no, their response was to put me on some of the less desirable work details, such as emptying and cleaning entire buses by myself.

One day about a month and a half into the job, the manager of the bus station called me into his office and told me that security people had been in the station at night, monitoring the building and watching what was going on.

They'd noticed that I wasn't playing the game.

And as a result, they cleared those guys out of the nest and made *me* the new supervisor.

What's my point? Well, the good that God put in me before any of that mess with the bus company began was used in startling ways. For me to move from the lowest job to the highest job in that bus station might have appeared to be an impossible task—except that God had already given me supervisory and leadership experience before I took the job. So it was a piece of cake.

Of course, much of my leadership ability grew *after* I gave my heart to the Lord and committed myself to serving Him. But what about the good that God puts in our lives *before* we even know Him well enough to call on His name?

AN AMAZING CHOICE

God puts good things into us when we're not even paying attention—He just does. And that's part of what's so amazing about the apostle Paul, the Christ-hater who became the number one spokesman for Christianity.

After Paul's incredible conversion, the Lord could have made it easy on Himself and just zapped Paul with a long list of great abilities—whatever he needed for doing what God had in mind. But instead, God reached back into a part of Paul's background that was pretty much formed *before* he became a Christian—and He found some very useful things there.

These were good things exactly as we defined *good* at the beginning of the book—those things that are helpful, beneficial, that keep you moving forward in life. They gave Paul a real jump start when God finally began to use him to set forth the Christian faith. And, just as may be the case with you, these qualities in Paul weren't all spiritual things. They were also academic, cultural, and biological.

These good things in Paul's life show up on his résumé in Philippians 3. Now, every one of us has gone in to apply for work, so we know what it means to present a résumé. A résumé lists the jobs you've had before—and that you've actually *had* a job (A résumé with no jobs listed isn't much of a résumé!)—and what your experiences have been.

It can also shed light on character issues, such as faithfulness. But perhaps most important, a résumé speaks of your *potential*. It ties things together and gives the appearance of continuity—and sometimes even purpose—to your life.

Paul's résumé is quite impressive. But again, remember that this is not the résumé of Paul *as a Christian*. This is his résumé *before* his conversion, before God grabbed him by the ears and remade everything about him.

BRAGGING RIGHTS

Paul begins his résumé by telling the Philippians: "I myself might have confidence even in the flesh. If anyone else has a mind to put confidence in the flesh, I far more" (Philippians 3:4). In other words, "Nobody has more to brag about than I do. When bragging rights go down in terms of human accomplishment, *I* am at the top of the list."

In fact, God seems to take particular delight in working huge miracles in the lives of the most unlikely people—which is exactly what He did with Paul. As I'm sure you'll remember, before Christ appeared to him on the road to Damascus and changed his heart, his mind, and his occupation—not to mention his name—Paul was actively engaged in the business of killing Christians.

Most of all, God massively changed Paul's spirit—from one that denied Christ to one that worshiped and exalted Him for all the remaining years of his life. And in the process, God used every good thing that was in Paul *before he became a Christian* to further His kingdom, even though those good things by themselves were not enough. In the same way, God can use every good thing that's true about you once you've committed yourself to Him as Paul did.

This brings me back to my starting point with Paul. Most people interpret Philippians 3:4 as an example of Paul's humility and his desire that others be humble as well. And it certainly is. But that same Scripture also demonstrates something else: Even though Paul seemed to be uniquely *unqualified* to work for God because of his monumental hatred for Christians, underneath all that garbage he was still uniquely qualified in a whole bunch of "good" ways. And those were the ways that God eventually used. Paul had it all—it just hadn't been sanctified yet (set apart for God's use). God wants to sanctify those good things in you.

A GOOD HOME

My own humble beginnings were quite different from Paul's. I was born and raised in inner-city Baltimore. By the time I was about ten, my parents were not getting along and from all appearances looked to be heading for divorce. But then one day everything changed: Someone witnessed to my father and he accepted Christ.

At first my mother hated the whole idea. She didn't like their life when my dad *wasn't* a Christian, and she liked it even less now that he *was*. After his conversion, my father developed the habit of getting up at midnight and praying that God would save my mother and the family. This went on for some time. Then one night my mother went downstairs to the living room, where Dad was praying.

She began crying even before she reached the living

room. When my father asked what was wrong, with anguished tears and a desperate heart she said the unforgettable: "The worse I am to you the better you are to me, so whatever you have must be real. How can I have it too?"

That night my father led my mother to Christ. Not too long after, my parents led their four kids to Christ too. I was the oldest. I was saved at eleven, felt the call to be a minister by the time I entered my teens, and was totally ministry-oriented by the time I hit eighteen.

Believe me, there was a world of difference between what went on in my home *before* we found the Lord and *after!*

But Paul never experienced the kind of before-and-after dichotomy that took place in my home. Paul was raised in a religious home, his parents following the law closely. To see what I'm driving at, let's look at what Paul mentions about himself. He says he was "circumcised the eighth day" (v. 5). In that era, Paul's circumcision represented the deep commitment of his mother and father to the Old Testament law. It means they were devout and started him off following the law early, pointing him down the right Jewish road. Paul is basically saying, "I was raised right, and my right rearing began on the eighth day after my birth."

Further on, Paul says that he was "of the nation of Israel" (v. 5). He was part of a race that was uniquely blessed by God. "I am of the nation of Israel; I'm Jewish." In other words, Paul was proud of his Jewish heritage because he considered it a direct link to God.

Now, given how much Paul changed after his Damascus Road encounter with Christ, you might argue that he didn't seem to know much about who God really was when he first started out. But that's not my point. God worked out the details to give this man a personal history that covered all the bases. And by doing that, God made Paul tremendously more effective when he was sent out to tell others about Christ.

SUPER JEW!

Next, Paul tells us that he was "of the tribe of Benjamin" (v. 5). Not only did he belong to the right race; he belonged to the right *class* in the right race. In that era if you were part of the tribe of Benjamin, you were living large.

The tribe of Benjamin had two fundamental characteristics. It was one of only two tribes from which a remnant remained faithful to God throughout Israel's history.

Those two tribes were Judah and Benjamin, which together made up the southern kingdom of Israel known as Judah.

Also, whenever the children of Israel went out to fight, the Benjamites went first because they were the bravest of the brave. That was their second major characteristic.

So Paul is telling the Philippians that he has good parental stock and good racial stock. Plus, he also comes from the crème de la crème within the race itself. He is a Hebrew among Hebrews. That means he was a super Jew. Paul says, "I'm a Jew and I'm proud! I'm not only a Hebrew among all those who are Hebrews; I am *the* Hebrew. I am *the man.*"

WHAT GOD LOOKS FOR

To finish his résumé, Paul says, "as to the Law, a Pharisee" (v. 5). This distinction had to do with Paul's vocation. He was a leader in the Sanhedrin, the ruling body in Israel. The guys he hung out with before his conversion were politicians and social scientists, and they were also students of the law.

That was why whenever Paul showed up in a new

town, the first place he went was the synagogue, to teach and debate with the leaders. He felt comfortable with them because he knew where they were coming from—he used to be one of them!

So Paul had a leadership role in society to go with the rest of his qualifications. Truly, in all the important ways—socially, academically, religiously—Paul was plugged in. He had climbed the ladder of success and was hanging out on the top rungs. And all of this before he even met Christ!

Now, what does any of that have to do with what God had in mind for Paul? Well,

- when God looked for a man to be an early leader in His church…
- when God looked for a man to write down the theology for His church…
- when God looked for a man who could debate the religious leaders that argued against His church…
- when God looked for a man who could advance the cause of Christ in academic and social arenas…
- when God looked for a man who could go all the way uptown to Caesar yet still go downtown and talk straight to the most hurting people…

…God found the man who already had all the necessary qualifications—and that man was Paul.

Paul had it all—it just hadn't been set apart for God's use. So God reached down, gave Paul his Damascus Road experience, then used all the things that were already there.

HOW CAN GOD USE *YOUR* LIFE?

Here's what I know is true about you:

Even before you were saved, God had already recognized all the good things about you. These qualifications included everything in your background—who your parents were, where they came from, where you got your education, how many years you spent in school, the jobs you had, the experience you acquired, the training you received.

They also included things that God put inside you at the moment of your birth, even those things that sometimes seemed to work against you as you were growing up. Do you hang on to ideas like a pit bull? God can use that. Do you love to pore through books and research what God has said? He can use that too. Are you quick to confront, eager to run right at the enemy and spit in his face? God can use that as well.

Because what God wants to do—or at least what He wants the *option* to do, once you commit yourself to Him as Paul did—is to sanctify those things that are already part of you so He can use them to advance His kingdom.

The question is: How will God use the good things that have happened in your life to promote His kingdom? How will He use the good things He put in you before you were born for His purposes?

SERVING WHERE GOD SENDS

A good friend of mine pastors a church in West Dallas. Some people in my friend's church started their own school for the poorest of the poorest of the poor. But they encountered a problem as they began to proceed with the school-development process: Nobody wanted to work at this school. Nobody wanted to teach at this school.

Most of the kids attending it came from single-parent homes, and many had financial problems that some of us, bad as it may get, couldn't even imagine. I saw lots of poverty growing up in Baltimore, but nothing like what these kids endured. I don't think I need to elaborate. You know the story—for most of these kids it was clearly a bad situation.

So the school needed a solid man with a solid heart for ministry who could meet these special needs. The school needed the best-of-the-best to work there because they had a worst-of-the-worst situation on their hands. They needed a headmaster with the eyes of a seer, feet that would go anywhere in the world, and a heart that would break in two for these kids.

So along came a gentleman who had a burden for kids. He had a passion for helping poor kids, but he was not a trained educator or administrator—he was a lawyer! He had graduated from one of the major law schools.

So this man had come forward but didn't have the training or education to take on an administrative position in the school. But as the folks involved with starting the school got deeper into the process, which involved buying property from the city and following a whole bunch of regulations, they realized that they needed legal advice.

Guess who offered to help them with the legal details facing the school? This gentleman with a heart for kids said, "Well, I can help you with the legal matters. Let me volunteer my time and use the training God has allowed me to get to help you buy this property and get all the clearances you need to become an official school. I'll handle all the legal details."

So he got involved with the folks at the school, dealing with the legalities.

But you know what? The other day the school put out a call for a headmaster, and wouldn't you know—because of all the legal issues the city was raising, to fill that job correctly, they needed somebody with legal expertise!

This godly man found out about their need and tossed and turned all night long. The next day he met with the people in charge and said, "I just can't shake this thing. If you want a lawyer who has a love for kids and who's willing to do this job, I will take it on. I believe that God is calling me to that."

They hired him, and he's serving there right now.

I'm sure he has a smile on his face, but if you could look inside him, I'm willing to bet you'd see an even bigger smile around his heart. Maybe even a little golden halo. Because here's a man who was led by God into a situation that God created him for long before that man ever knew what God really had in mind.

NO WASTE WITH GOD

God is not going to waste anything He can use! He's not going to waste anything He created.

Paul had all the raw ingredients. God decided to use those, and that was good. Likewise, the headmaster at that new school had all the raw ingredients for God's purpose. And quite frankly, neither one of those men would have predicted how things eventually turned out. If you'd caught up with either one of them when they were twenty-five years old and asked them what the future held, I'm sure their answers would have been entirely different from what they actually ended up doing.

You see, the principle is the same for everyone—whether God created you for something local or global, temporary or permanent, small or large, hidden or out in the open…

- God *prepares* you,
- God *positions* you, and
- God *enables* you to do what He knows you can do most effectively.

And almost always it's the one thing in the world that will make you completely happy as well, although you don't always know that in advance.

When I was called into the manager's office at the bus company that morning so many years ago, I had no idea that the good in me was about to be used. Before that day, I'd had a horrible sense of fear about how the unscrupulous acts of those employees would come out and who would be hurt by all the cheating.

But God had *prepared* me by making sure that I'd had experience in leadership roles before. He'd also prepared me by teaching me right from wrong, through parents who had learned the difference themselves.

He had *positioned* me in exactly the right place at exactly the right time to do what He had prepared me for.

And He had *enabled* me by giving me the strength to stand against the crowd.

You might be able to relate—initially feeling like you're in the wrong place at the wrong time, then finding out that God put you there for a reason, to use you for His purposes. Are you in a situation like that right now, wondering how in the world you're going to make a way for yourself, dig yourself out of that hole, turn it around for good? You're not alone. God is molding you and shaping you through this, preparing, positioning, and enabling you for great things that you can't even imagine.

You see, that's how God uses the good in us, both what He puts there by Himself and what He helps us develop. It's really a simple dynamic: *You get ready and God gets busy.*

Chapter 3

MISTAKES
INTO MIRACLES

ONE OF THE GREAT THINGS ABOUT GOD'S grace has to do with mistakes and failures. Going back to our definitions of *good, bad,* and *ugly,* mistakes and failures are what we might call bad things. And yet whether you made these mistakes when you were a non-Christian or a Christian, God can take your mistakes and turn them into miracles.

But I don't want anyone to go around misquoting

me. God doesn't endorse intentional sin! He doesn't say, "That's all right—go out and make all the mistakes you can so I'll have lots of raw material to work with. Then I can use you even more!"

On the contrary, Romans 6:1 says, "What shall we say then? Are we to continue in sin so that grace may increase?" We don't have some kind of license to sin just because we know God is gracious. God forbid. And you can't jive God—He requires *genuine* repentance, not conditional repentance built on false intent. You can't take God for a ride and manipulate His goodness.

Yet the reality is that God *can* take sins that we have truly repented of and use them to make us better people. More important, He can use those sins to better equip us to do what He wants us to do. And that's good news.

So…have *you* ever made any mistakes you regret?

Dumb question, right? Don't be asking me that question, or I'll bend your ear all day! *I've made mistakes, all right.*

I've even made mistakes in businesses I never should have been involved with in the first place, including at least one investment that wiped out what little cash reserve my wife, Lois, and I had at a time when we couldn't afford to be doing anything the least bit stupid with our money. That's all the detail I'm going to give you, except for one more fact. I did the whole thing—signed up, put in the money, and lost every cent—totally against my wife's wishes.

But we recovered and my wife forgave me. And I even learned something in the process. The trick is to let God use your mistakes to *improve* you rather than letting the devil use them to *destroy* you.

MR. FULL-SPEED-AHEAD!

We could talk about a lot of people in the Bible, but the one who gets my vote every time is Peter. Peter is my favorite because he was always talking and always right up front with everything. Remember? But also, here's a guy who had only one gear in his transmission: over-drive, full speed ahead. He wouldn't let anybody else out-energize him—Peter was always in charge, always wide open, always in the middle of whatever was going on. He's the kind of guy you'd want on your team when things are looking tough.

And yet Peter wasn't always on top of things. Luke 22 tells the story of the Last Supper, after which Jesus talked to His disciples for quite a while, knowing that this would be His last chance to make some points that He really wanted to bring home before His crucifixion. He also spoke directly to Peter. Jesus begins by saying, "Simon, Simon" (v. 31).

Now, Peter's full name was Simon Peter, so Jesus' words immediately suggest something to me. Whenever God calls your name twice, you know you're in trouble! Either that, or He's about to tell you something you don't want to hear. It's just like when your mama calls you by your first name *and* middle name—you know you're in for something!

"Simon, Simon, behold, Satan has demanded permission to sift you like wheat" (v. 31). In other words, Jesus is telling Peter: "Satan has come to Me and asked if he can have you." But that's not all Jesus said: "But I have prayed for you, that your faith may not fail" (v. 32). "Peter, I'm praying that you won't quit on Me." Isn't that an amazing realization? Even when you're not praying for yourself, Jesus is praying for you.

Then Jesus goes on: "And you, when once you have turned again, strengthen your brothers" (v. 32). Christ is saying to Peter that Satan has something in store for him. He even tells Peter that Satan will be allowed to get through to him, at least up to a point. "Once you have turned again" implies that Peter will indeed be sifted but will turn back to the Lord.

Yet through it all, Christ will be praying for Peter. First, He will pray that Peter's faith will not fail. Second, He will pray that no matter what Peter might do in a moment of weakness, once his faith has reasserted itself, he will use that experience to strengthen his brothers in Christ.

GOD ALWAYS DOES THE UNEXPECTED

Now when you think about this encounter, wouldn't you expect Jesus to say, "Hey, Peter, you're going to mess up, boy, so you've got to find someplace to hide"? But that's not what He says at all! He says, "Satan is coming after you…but I'm praying for you. And even though you will fail Me, when you get back on track, I want you to do something good with what's happened." That's the down-home version, but that's exactly what Christ laid out for Peter.

If Christ had said this to one of us, I'm sure we would have gritted our teeth and said, "No, it's not going to happen! I won't mess this up. Now that I know what's coming, I'll be ready!"

And that's exactly what Peter says in verse 33: "Lord, with You I am ready to go both to prison and to death!" In other words, "No failure here, Jesus. I'm your main man. You can be cool and depend on me. I am not going to fail, all right? In fact, I am so committed that I'd die before I mess up!"

But Jesus knew better.

"I say to you, Peter, the rooster will not crow today until you have denied three times that you know Me" (v. 34). In other words, "Not only are you going to mess up, Peter; you're going to mess up *before* tomorrow morning. And you will fail Me *three separate times*. But, then, when you turn around and get yourself back together, I will still have a ministry for you. And it'll be a ministry for which you alone will be qualified."

Christ intended to use Peter's unique experience to strengthen his Christian brothers—to use Peter's failure to produce good things.

NEVER UNDERESTIMATE GOD

So the question is, if temporary failure happened to Peter, one of Christ's handpicked disciples, how much more likely is it to happen to you? And when it does, what do you suppose the Lord wants to accomplish through it?

In general, you don't hear a lot of people asking that question. Instead, you hear people say things like, "Don't get into messes" and "Don't sin." Now, this is good advice—God doesn't want you sinning. But I believe that people should say, "Don't walk headfirst into sin when you know better. But when you fail, as you most surely will, let God use those failures for His glory."

Satan wants to sift you and me like wheat, just as he sifted Peter—but *God always has the upper hand.* God turned His Son's so-called defeat on the cross into Satan's biggest defeat in the history of the universe. And He turned what looked like a failure in Peter, one of Christ's twelve chosen apostles, into a whole string of evangelistic triumphs over Satan later on.

That's what you need to remember when things look bad: *God can take your most monstrous failures and turn them into triumphs such as you never could imagine.*

And one more thing—God isn't likely to think you're worth sifting if you aren't doing something right in the first place. Sifting is a way of purifying, of straining out the junk and refining what's left. That means there has to be something worth salvaging in you in the first place.

You could also look at it from another angle—Satan doesn't come looking to bother his friends. He has no need whatsoever to harass the ones who are already on his side.

Either way, to be tested because you're connected directly to God is an honor.

THE MORNING AFTER

Let's take a look at Peter's moment of failure. I suspect that you know this story pretty well already, but let's take another look.

First, a servant girl said to Peter, "Hey, you were with Jesus."

Peter replied, "Jesus? Jesus who? I don't know what you're talking about."

Then another girl said, "Wait a minute…! I know you were with Jesus because you're the dude that cut off my cousin's ear. I ain't going to forget the one who cut off my cousin's ear!"

"I told you—I don't know who He is!"

Finally other folks standing around the fire, warming their hands, said, "Yeah, yeah…you're one of the guys we saw with Jesus." And for the third time, Peter said, "I told you—it wasn't me! Somebody's gonna get hurt in here, because I told you I was never with Him!"

Cock-a-doodle-doo!

Peter realized at that instant that Jesus' words from the night before were true. "Immediately, while he was still speaking, a rooster crowed" (Luke 22:60). And then, "The Lord turned and looked at Peter. And Peter remembered the word of the Lord, how He had told him, 'Before a rooster crows today, you will deny Me three times.' And he went out and wept bitterly" (vv. 61–62).

You don't see much greater failure than this. You can't be much more out in the open than to deny the Lord publicly.

Yet Jesus knew *in advance* what Peter would do. Nevertheless, He didn't stop him. He simply told him, "When you get back to your senses, you'll be useful again in My kingdom."

And as we know from Scripture, that's what happened.

Do you understand what's going on here? Do you understand that God can take the bad, when it's repented of, and make you more useful? That doesn't excuse the bad, and it certainly doesn't wipe out the consequences.

But it does mean that God is bigger than our human failures.

Jesus is *always* more ready to forgive than you are to confess. Buildings fall apart; they collapse and leave messes. But one of the major wonders of your Christian life is that Jesus Christ can take the rubble left by those messes—those awful, useless leftovers—and construct something entirely new. And beautiful.

Peter promised never to forsake Jesus, but by the time the rooster crowed, he'd already done it three times. When does the rooster crow? Early in the morning, right? So that means that the rooster crowed at the beginning of a brand-new day. When he crows after a night of failure, that means the sun has just come up. One of my friends says, "Every time I get to midnight, God gives me another day." In Peter's case, that "another day" dawned after the night of his greatest failure—yet God blessed him with a new day to do what was right, to repent of his sin, and to go on because of that sin and do even greater things for the Lord.

FAILURE TRANSFORMED

Chuck Colson was squarely in the middle of the Watergate conspiracy that unfolded during the 1970s. He was Richard Nixon's "hatchet man" and was deeply involved in all kinds of illegal stuff, for which he eventually went to prison. But through a series of events that he had no idea was coming down, he came face-to-face with Jesus Christ and was gloriously transformed.

After serving his time in prison, he was given a burden for other prisoners—men and women he never would have encountered except for his own sin. Now prisoners all over the world have been saved by the thousands through an organization called Prison Fellowship, which Chuck Colson started.

God took the bad in Colson's life and turned it completely around.

But again, let's be clear. God didn't want Chuck Colson to go to prison in the first place! That wasn't God's idea; He wasn't happy to see that man break the law and fall into sin. But when it happened, God took Chuck Colson's failure and turned it into a blessing for a lot of other people. He turned it totally around.

GOD IS NO PUSHOVER

After his sin with Bathsheba and repentance, David said, "Restore to me the joy of Your salvation and sustain me with a willing spirit. Then I will teach transgressors Your ways, and sinners will be converted to You" (Psalm 51:12–13).

I'll say it again: That doesn't mean David's sin was somehow productive in some honorable way and therefore all right with God. You can't play with God. You can't con Him and you can't push Him into a corner. You can't say, "Well, since the best way to know how sin works is to go astray, let me go as far out there as possible so I can learn the max!" No, God never wants you to sin, but He knows that you will and offers hope despite that sin. But after David's failure and after God restored David to Himself, he went on to teach others about God's ways.

What's amazing is that the grace of God is so far-reaching and profound that *He can use your failures.*

MIRACLES APPLIED

So what does that mean for you, right here and now? It means you should seek God's mercy. Give Him your lemons and let Him make lemonade. Give Him the things in your life that aren't so good, the things you're not so proud of, and say, "Lord, here they are. I wish my life were different, but it's not. I wish I could change it, but I can't."

And then let God go to work.

Hand your mess over to God. Tell Him, "If Your grace can get in here and tweak and twist and turn this mess around, I'm available for You to use me for something better. I acknowledge that it's *my* mess, *my* fault, but I give it over to You to do with as You wish."

I've said it before and I'll say it again: If we let Him work, God doesn't waste a thing. And if you give Him a chance, He certainly won't waste you—He's up to something great in your life.

Chapter 4

GOD HAS
A BETTER IDEA

I WAS RAISED IN MARYLAND, one of the few eastern states that still offered duckpin bowling during that time. Duckpin bowling is similar to regular bowling, except the balls are only about five inches in diameter and the pins are only nine to ten inches tall. The alley itself is basically the same as a typical bowling alley.

In those days, the automatic pin-setting machines were not as reliable as they are today and would often miss a pin or two when they reset the pins. So there was always a guy in the background, sitting on a high bench built into the wall behind the lane, who would hop down and reset any pins the machine missed.

But no one ever got to see his face. If your own brother worked there, you couldn't prove it from what you could observe, unless he wore neon shoes that no one else could match. All anyone ever saw from the front were legs, feet, and sometimes hands.

Many times, God is like that. When the pins in your life are getting knocked down all over the landscape, you can't always see Him in the background. But He's still there, setting them back up, getting ready for you to roll again.

The way He constantly works in the background also applies to all the unique things that make you different from anyone else, the things that often seem the most difficult for God to use.

These are the things we call "ugly." The negative things that have happened to you that you had no control over and that have marked your life indelibly. If God's grace weren't available, these ugly things would be like graffiti that won't wash off, written on your soul with permanent spray paint. But as always, God is in charge, finding ways even when you can't see Him working at all.

ONE OF THE MAJOR UGLIES

Let's look at an example of how God often works—so quietly that you can't see or hear Him at all in the background. One-fourth of the book of Genesis is given over to a young man named Joseph. You wanna talk about not fair? What happened to Joseph was *not fair* no matter how you slice it. But God did some incredible things through that man, which we'll come to in a moment.

Joseph was born into what we would call a dysfunctional family, all right? We don't have space to go into all the details about Joseph's life here; you can read the whole story in Genesis, starting at chapter 37. But believe me, Joseph came from a dysfunctional home!

Jacob, Joseph's father, was a shyster, a trickster from the time he was a little boy. He was always running a game. In cahoots with his mother, Jacob cheated his own brother, Esau, out of his birthright by tricking his father. And this was in a day when a person's birthright meant practically everything to the next generation. A father's official blessing, which by tradition always went to the first male child, carried huge bragging rights, not to mention the property inheritance that went along with it.

So you have Jacob's mother working against her own husband to trick him into giving the birthright to the wrong son, the younger son. Jacob learned from his mother and learned well. He caught on to this kind of thing as a youngster, and he got good at it. And much of his life involved one conniving after another. But eventually he settled down and had a family, Joseph being the eleventh son.

So Joseph had ten older brothers, and let me tell you that these guys were a trip! Some of them were murderers—they'd kill you as quick as look at you. One had an affair with his father's concubine. Another had sex with his daughter-in-law, mistaking her for a prostitute. I mean, it's all kinds of crazy stuff.

"DAD LOVES YOU BEST!"

Joseph never asked to be born into such a family. He had no choice. So how did he deal with it? How did he process those ugly circumstances—*ugly* things—that came crashing into his life, every single one of them as ugly as anything that could ever happen to you and me?

Well, Joseph triumphed in the end because he served God in spite of all that was done to him. He wasn't perfect at every single moment but acted to the best of the ability God gave him.

Joseph's story began with a particular trigger event that happened when he was still a young boy. Genesis 37:3 says, "Now Israel [Jacob] loved Joseph more than all his sons, because he was the son of his old age; and he made him a varicolored tunic." Joseph had probably been Jacob's favorite son since the day he was born. So when Jacob showed his preference by giving Joseph a fancy coat, it nearly pushed his already jealous and angry brothers over the edge.

Joseph's ten older brothers had already seen that their father loved Joseph more than he loved any of them. And they hated Joseph all the more and "could not speak to him on friendly terms" (v. 4). That's called sibling rivalry, brought on in this case by favoritism shown by the father. And it was a serious case of sibling rivalry in this family— not just fighting over whose turn it is with the Game Boy, but fighting to the death.

To make matters worse, little Joseph seemed totally oblivious to all this ill will among his brothers. Not only did he rat out his brothers for doing a poor job in the field; he also had a dream in which his brothers were all binding sheaves in the field, and he just *insisted* on telling them about it: "Please listen to this dream which I have had; for behold, we were binding sheaves in the field, and lo, my sheaf rose up and also stood erect; and behold, your sheaves gathered around and bowed down to my sheaf" (vv. 6–7).

This was not a good story to be telling people who already hated you! Joseph's dreams, combined with the gift of the multicolored coat from his father and the unequal treatment that had gone on before, finally provoked the other brothers' jealousy to a critical point.

And that led to a plan to kill Joseph.

Now, things gotta be pretty bad if your own brothers want to wipe you out. Yet even then, God had His hand in things. Reuben, one of Jacob's other sons, took pity on Joseph and talked the gang into throwing Joseph into a pit rather than killing him outright. The pit had no water, so Joseph would probably die of thirst or exposure anyway, which worked for the other brothers. But Reuben planned to go back to the pit and rescue Joseph as soon as the other brothers were gone.

But Reuben never got the chance to follow through with his plan, though his intervention still saved Joseph's life. While the brothers were eating their lunch (Can you imagine breaking out the cookies with your own brother trapped in a pit just a few yards away?), a caravan of Midianite traders came along, heading south to Egypt. Suddenly the brothers saw an even better way to be rid of Joseph without having his blood on their hands—at least in a literal sense. They also saw a chance to make a little money on the side. So they lifted Joseph out of the pit and sold him to the traders for twenty shekels of silver.

TALK ABOUT COLD-BLOODED

Now that's cold—not as cold as killing him outright, but still cold-blooded. Joseph's own brothers sold him into slavery, out of jealousy, because their father liked Joseph more than he liked them. Here we have a really bad family background, just the opposite of Paul's, yet God used this whole affair in a mighty way.

Many of you have come from bad family backgrounds too. And many of you are in pain today because of what Mama was like, what Daddy was like, what your brothers and sisters were like. And many of you are still enduring that pain. Maybe abuse by a father. Maybe neglect. Maybe rejection.

In my years as a pastor, I've heard every story you could imagine about rejection and abuse. Maybe a few stories you *couldn't* imagine. But of all the terrible things I've heard, all the awful things I've encountered, I believe that sexual abuse of children is the most grievous, not only because of the horrific effects that kind of abuse often has on the victims, but also because of the punishment God has promised: "But whoever causes one of these little ones who believe in Me to stumble, it would be better for him to have a heavy millstone hung around his neck, and to be drowned in the depth of the sea" (Matthew 18:6).

Yet I know one lady who was horribly abused as a child and was able, with God's help, to turn those awful, ugly experiences over to Him. In return, He healed her spirit and gave her an incredible affinity for other kids. Out of the horrible desolation of that experience, God called this woman to work with children, which she has been doing for many years.

Now, that's not the kind of abuse Joseph endured, but nevertheless, he got a terrible deal. How much worse can it get than being sold as a slave—as a nothing, a nobody? And by your own family! You talk about a self-image problem—that could create a real self-image problem. *I must be a nobody,* Joseph probably thought. What else would most people think? In one afternoon, Joseph went from favored son to slave.

To cover their tracks, the brothers put blood from an animal all over Joseph's coat, the multicolored coat Jacob had given him, and took it back to Jacob, who immediately went into mourning, assuming that his favorite son had been eaten by a wild beast.

Meanwhile, when Joseph got to Egypt, the Midianites sold him as a slave in the home of a man named Potiphar, one of Pharaoh's highest ranking officials, the captain of his bodyguard. So Joseph has been betrayed by his own brothers and sold into slavery. Even so, Genesis tells us that *the Lord was with Joseph:*

> It came about that from the time [Potiphar] made him overseer in his house and over all that he owned, the LORD blessed the Egyptian's house on account of Joseph; thus the LORD's blessing was upon all that he owned, in the house and in the field. (Genesis 39:5)

NO MATTER HOW UGLY THE PAIN...

Do you see the good news in this passage? Here's the first part: *No matter what your background or how deep the pain you've been through, the Lord will be with you.*

God can take that rejection, that pain, that hurt, all those psychological difficulties by whatever fancy name you might call them, and still do something with them in your life, no matter how ugly the whole mess might be.

It doesn't matter whether all that stuff is caused by dysfunction in your family, other people's sins, or anything else that's basically not your fault. It qualifies as ugly, but God can make it good. And right here is your proof—God was with Joseph, who was in a worse situation than most of us will ever endure, and yet the Lord blessed him.

You might know the next part of the story. Potiphar's wife began to lust after Joseph. The Bible tells us why she liked him: He "was handsome in form and appearance" (39:6). He looked *good*. Whether he worked out at his neighborhood gym every day we don't really know—maybe hard work did as much for his physical body as two hours a day at Gold's Gym. All we know is that the boy was tight.

And Potiphar's wife wasn't blind. She propositioned

Joseph about as boldly as a person can: "Come to bed with me!"

Joseph's response was not what she expected.

> But he refused and said to his master's wife, "Behold, with me here, my master does not concern himself with anything in the house, and he has put all that he owns in my charge. There is no one greater in this house than I, and he has withheld nothing from me except you, because you are his wife. How then could I do this great evil and sin against God?" (39:8–9)

That last line certainly bears repeating: "How then could I do this great evil and sin against God?" That's another book all by itself! But Potiphar's wife didn't give up. She caught Joseph by his robe one day and tried to drag him into her bedroom. Instead, he slipped his arms out and made for the door. But later that day, she falsely accused him in front of her husband, and Potiphar threw Joseph into prison. He went to jail because of an ugly, ugly lie.

GOD'S BETTER IDEA

You know, it's bad enough to have your family mess over you as a kid, but now Joseph was grown and couldn't even go to work and do a good job without having the boss's wife working against him! Now he was in jail, and the man hadn't done a thing wrong.

In fact, Joseph did the *right* thing when he refused Potiphar's wife and asked how he could do such a thing and sin against God. But for a while, doing the right thing didn't seem to do Joseph any good, an experience that is not completely uncommon. Sometimes in the short run, doing right can cost you in a lot of different ways.

I can tell you from my experience at the bus company that doing the right thing was expensive for me at the time. When I refused to participate in the time-clock scam, it hurt—it cost me so-called friends, it cost me time, and it caused me a lot of anxiety. Also I had to work a lot harder than anyone else. My coworkers piled on the work and left me to do it alone. I also had to endure a lot of nasty talk and even a few confrontations that left me feeling pretty miserable. Yet during that time, *the Lord was with me,* just like He was with Joseph.

From my work as a pastor, I also know that most of

you could tell the same kind of stories. On occasion everyone endures pain because of choosing to do the right thing. Yet God always has something better in mind! And besides, who said life would always be fair in the short run? Many times that's when you really need to hang on.

But the Lord is always with us; He never lets us get in too far over our heads. Sometimes, though, we go through tough times so we can come out at the other end stronger than ever. *God always has something better in mind.*

Chapter 5

WHAT'S
NOT FAIR?

WE ENDED THE LAST CHAPTER with Joseph in a situation that was totally unfair. When you think about it, though, Joseph's situation probably isn't *that* unusual. Anybody else ever been lied to? Cheated out of something? Talked about behind your back? If you have—and *everyone* has—then you know what Joseph was going through.

But you know what? Exactly as you might expect, while Joseph was in prison, *the Lord was still with him* (see Genesis 39:21–23). And before long, as the Lord granted Joseph favor in the eyes of the warden, he was put in charge of all the prisoners and everything that was done in that prison.

Nowadays we might call that position sort of a supertrusty (a prisoner who is considered trustworthy and is given special privileges), but the Bible doesn't give us a specific name for Joseph's new job. It just says that he was so dependable that the warden paid no attention at all to what he did. Joseph trusted the Lord, and because God was with him and granted him favor, the warden trusted Joseph.

Before long, two other very important guys, who had gotten into some trouble with Pharaoh, came along and were put under Joseph's care. The king of Egypt, the Pharaoh, was furious with these two officials, the chief cupbearer (like a butler) and the chief baker, because they had offended him. So he tossed them into confinement, and they ended up under Joseph's authority (see Genesis 40:1–4).

THE RIGHT QUESTIONS

When things get ugly, the question you should ask is not "Why am I going through this?" but "Lord, how do You want to use this ugliness to move me ahead for Your purposes?" It's important to ask the right question because if you don't, you get frustrated. You can't afford to take the "It's not fair!" approach instead of the "Lord, You must be up to something great!" approach. Trust me, when you begin to ask the right question, the answers will become much easier to find.

Let me tell you about a time when I got mad at the Lord and then took some time before I got around to asking the right questions. That's right—I was *mad!* Not mad enough to kick tires and smash windows, but certainly ticked off. Mad, that is, until I suddenly saw the far better thing God had in mind for me.

At that time my family was driving a 1970 Pontiac Grand Prix. Now, that was a good car when it was new, but at the time of this story, believe me, it wasn't 1970 anymore! Our neighbors knew we were on the way home ten minutes before we came in sight. I'm talking about *noise*—a lot of noise. And it wasn't the muffler either; that car just had a lot of rattles and squeaks, along with a few pops and mini-explosions that no one but a mechanic could hope to identify. It had a language of sputters and gasps, and a modus operandi all its own.

But no matter how bad that car needed work—and,

trust me, it needed work—every month we gave fifty dollars to the Lord before we bought anything else, including having work done on our only form of transportation. At that time we had a monthly income of just $350, so that fifty dollars represented somewhat more than a normal tithe. But we were committed to giving that amount—we had made a covenant with God, which we wouldn't break no matter what.

One Sunday morning when we left for church, all I had in my pocket was fifty dollars. We needed groceries, but that fifty dollars was God's money, not ours. So we dropped it into the collection plate even as we breathed a prayer: *That's it, Lord—we are choosing to trust You!*

A few days later we were on the freeway when thick clouds of black smoke began pouring out from under the hood. One way or another we managed to pull over without hitting anyone else, got the fire put out, and had that wretched car towed to the mechanic's place. I must tell you that as we walked out of the auto repair shop, I was ticked off at God.

Lord, we don't even have bus money home! We just gave You our last fifty dollars on Sunday. Is this fair?

Early the next day, knowing full well that our insurance had a two-hundred-dollar deductible, I caught a ride back to the repair shop to try to fix this seemingly unfixable situation. I was plenty discouraged, believe me. I was also fully aware that I had to make some kind of a decision that day, and I didn't know what in the world to do. But before I could make a move, I had to know how bad the damage was.

Imagine my surprise when I walked in the door and saw my car in the service bay, hood off, half the engine stripped out, and mechanics going like gangbusters to put in new parts and tune everything up. Panicked, I grabbed the first guy with a clipboard who crossed my path.

"You can't be doing that! Have you talked to my insurance company? I have a two-hundred-dollar deductible, and I can't pay it!"

He smiled. "That's right, my friend. You *do* have a two-hundred-dollar deductible, but we talked to them this morning, and they gave us the okay to go ahead and get this car back on the road. Have you read the fine print in your policy?"

It didn't take me long to get my policy out, and there it was in black and white: We did have a two-hundred-dollar deductible—*except for fire*. If the car went up in flames, the damage was covered, 100 percent.

I can tell you, we had church in the repair shop that day.

THINGS CAN ALWAYS GET UGLIER

Now, this might sound crazy at first, but I think Joseph was put into a situation very similar to mine. The details were different but the dynamics were basically the same—he was in a difficult position that wasn't his own fault. But instead of getting ticked off at what looked like a wrecking ball to the head, Joseph said something like this:

"Lord, if You had to allow whatever's going on in my life so You could bring about an even greater thing, that's okay. I don't deserve this, but I am willing to put my very life in Your hands—especially since I know You must be up to something good!"

We don't know for sure what Joseph actually did, except that he served diligently and was given charge of the prison. Before long, both the cupbearer and baker who were put in jail with him had a dream on the same night. And both of them needed someone to tell them what their dreams meant. That person was Joseph, for God had given him the ability to interpret dreams.

For the baker, the news was bad; within three days he

would be hanged. But for the cupbearer, the news was just the opposite. Joseph told him that within three days he would be taken out of prison and sent back to his former job.

Then, when he finished the cupbearer's interpretation, Joseph added a little plea for himself. "When you go up to see Pharaoh," he said, "would you kindly remember me to him? Because I shouldn't be in here. Keep me in mind when it goes well with you" (see Genesis 40:14–15).

It was a great idea, but…in his elation over his release and reinstatement, the cupbearer forgot all about Joseph. For years!

For Joseph, life was getting uglier fast! He thought he'd finally found a way out. You find a homeboy in jail, and the homeboy gets his freedom—and then he forgets who he knew when he was back in jail! How unfair can this get? Can you imagine what Joseph must have gone through?

DREAMWORKS IN THE OLD TESTAMENT

But again, God wasn't done. The Lord was with Joseph. Two long, difficult, draggin'-on years later, Pharaoh had two different dreams on the same night that scared him half to death. He didn't understand either one and needed someone to interpret them.

And that's when the chief cupbearer remembered something way back in his past. "Oh yeah, there was this guy in prison named Joseph. And he was *good* with dreams! I don't know if you want to talk to him, but if you bring him out, he might be able to help."

Pharaoh agreed to bring in Joseph because none of his own people could make heads or tails of what he had dreamed. So Joseph came and listened to Pharaoh's dreams. Pharaoh had seen seven fat cows devoured by seven lean cows and seven healthy heads of grain swallowed up by seven scrawny heads.

Through divine revelation directly from God, Joseph told Pharaoh that his dreams both meant the same thing: Egypt would be blessed with seven years of abundance followed by seven years of famine.

Then Joseph went one step further and told Pharaoh what he should do. "Store one-fifth of all the grain that grows in Egypt during the years of abundance," he said, "and use this reserve during the years of famine to keep Egypt from being destroyed" (see Genesis 41:34–36).

Pharaoh was impressed! "Since God has informed

you of all this, there is no one so discerning and wise as you are. You shall be over my house, and according to your command all my people shall do homage; only in the throne I will be greater than you" (vv. 39–40).

MOVING ON UP

Talk about going from the outhouse to the White House! In the space of about thirty minutes, Joseph went from the number two spot in a tiny jail to the number two spot in all of Egypt. And what God was able to do as a result of that instantaneous promotion had ramifications that go on yet today, almost four thousand years later.

First, Joseph became the means of salvation from famine for Jacob and the rest of his family, who were God's own people, by providing grain and keeping them alive through the seven years of famine.

Second, out of Joseph's humble beginnings God was then able, through Moses and all the leaders who followed him, to preserve the nation of Israel all the way through to the present day.

Third, all this includes that little trip, through the lineage of David, to the Cross on Calvary and the person of Jesus Christ Himself.

And all because Joseph was faithful to the God of his fathers and was honored by the Lord in return.

Meanwhile, back in Canaan, Joseph's father and his eleven brothers (another brother had been born after Joseph was sold into slavery) eventually began to starve because of the famine foretold by Joseph. But the word got out that Egypt had grain. And Jacob eventually had no choice but to send his sons down to Egypt to buy some.

Little did Joseph's brothers know whom they were buying grain from when they arrived. They hadn't seen Joseph in years, and by then he'd grown into a man, probably with a fancy headdress and a smooth chin. But Joseph recognized them right away, and strangely enough, he was overwhelmed with love in spite of what they'd done to him so long ago.

But he still had a question or two to settle. Before he could reveal who he was, he had to know what kind of men they were at this point in their lives. Were they as mean as ever, or had they changed?

Likewise, God needs to know what kind of man or woman you are before He can usher you into the place He's created you for. Or into the place He's created *for you.*

WHAT DID GOD CREATE *YOU* FOR?

I'm sometimes known as a preacher with a *big* voice. Not a big mouth, I hope, but a big voice! When I'm in the pulpit and the Lord lays a message on my heart, I get excited, and sometimes that excitement comes through in my delivery.

But my voice, strong or weak as it might be, wasn't always entirely usable. I was born a stutterer. I can't tell you how long and how hard I had to work to overcome that problem. I knew that God had called me to be a minister, to preach the gospel, and I knew that I had to get my speaking voice under some kind of control.

Boy, did God make it hard for me! Many times I wondered if I'd ever get out seven words in a row. I think the people around me wondered even more. But somehow I always believed that God gave me that difficulty to surmount for a very specific reason: He was testing me, finding out if I'd do the necessary work to come into the territory He'd ordained for me. He knew if I'd stake it out then, I'd stick it out later—and He was right.

Like Joseph, like me, and like just about every other long-term Christian I've ever met, you might be called to be refined through testing and trials. God can't give stainless steel assignments to cast iron people.

Chapter 6

NEVER TOO LATE
FOR GOD

ONCE JOSEPH HAD TESTED HIS BROTHERS and deter-
mined that their hearts had truly changed, he identified
himself to them:

> "I am your brother Joseph, whom you sold into
> Egypt. Now do not be grieved or angry with
> yourselves, because you sold me here, *for God
> sent me before you to preserve life.* For the famine

has been in the land these two years, and there
are still five years in which there will be neither
plowing nor harvesting. God sent me before you
to preserve for you a remnant in the earth, and
to keep you alive by a great deliverance."
(Genesis 45:4–7, emphasis added)

I added the italics to point out what Joseph was really
trying to communicate to his brothers. But wait a
minute, you say. How could Joseph be telling his brothers that God *sent* him? He was sold into slavery. Potiphar
bought him. He was accused of rape. He was put in jail.
The cupbearer forgot about him.

That's human interpretation. Let me tell you the real
deal, as Joseph himself might have phrased it.

The important thing is not that you sold me into
slavery. God sent me down here before you to
save your lives! You thought you were getting rid
of me, yet God was orchestrating a plan, using
negative, ugly events because He had a purpose
that no one could have guessed in advance.

He made me for this moment! And now my
moment has come.

IT'S NEVER TOO LATE FOR GOD

The point of this entire story of Joseph and his brothers, at least as far as you and I are concerned, comes in Genesis 50:20 when Joseph says, "You meant evil against me, but God meant it for good."

If you have ugliness in your life, believe me, you're not alone. I can't tell you how many folks have said to me that their mama didn't treat them right, their daddy didn't treat them right, their brothers didn't treat them right, their boss didn't treat them right. And maybe you're like that—maybe you've been juked and jived and scorned as sure as you were born.

But in spite of all that, that doesn't mean someone else's action against you is the bottom line. Most of the time, God doesn't purposely send ugly events our way, but when they happen He doesn't freak out either. The reason is simple: He knows that somewhere down the line He'll be able to use all that ugly stuff to bring your life into focus and straighten you out.

It's never too late for God!

And when He does turn all your ugliness around, you'll be qualified to go out and save the life of someone else who's been abused and broken and put in a lot of pain. That's exactly what Joseph did, that's exactly what the lady who had been abused did, and that's exactly what you can do.

SEE IT AS GOD SEES IT

Many times it helps if, right up front, you can learn to see your pain as God sees it. Don't just say, "That's not fair!" Say, "God, since that's not fair—and it's *not* fair—what are You going to do to help me turn it around? I give You the right to take my ugliness and use it for Your glory!"

If you start from that mindset, you will arrive at an entirely different place.

Let me give you a totally different image to make the same point. Have you ever been to a *real* pizzeria? I'm not talking about the kind of place where everything is pre-measured and prepackaged and premade and the whole process is broken down into simple, foolproof steps. Those pizza places can train a thirteen-year-old who's never heard the word *knead* in his entire life to make what they call "perfect pizza" every time.

No, what I'm talking about is a real pizzeria, the kind of place where they take a ball of dough, slam it down, and roll that baby around. Okay, you with me? They pound that piece of dough. They twirl that baby. That piece of dough goes through a whole lot of grief before it gets rolled out.

You know why? Because the good stuff—and I'm talking now about the sauce and the anchovies (well, maybe we'd want to hold the anchovies) and the pepperoni and the sausage, the good stuff—has to have something strong to lay on top of. So they take that dough and brutalize it—beat it, roll it, twirl it, slap it, and beat it some more. And finally, they spin it out and make it big enough to hold all the good stuff they plan to put on top.

Think of yourself as that pizza dough and God as the Person working that dough. God's got some good stuff He wants to lay on you, but before He can give you that good stuff, He has to start you out as a ball of dough. He has to roll you and pound you and twist you and spin you out so that when it comes time for the good stuff, there'll be something to put it on top of—something strong enough to really *hold* all that good stuff.

God has a purpose for you, but He means to pound you into the place where the good stuff can lay on top of you, so that everybody who sees you following His purpose will say, "Uh-huh, that's good. That's the real thing!"

That's what God has in store for you.

Chapter 7

"I HAVE A PLAN FOR YOU"

GOD HAS A PLAN FOR YOUR LIFE. Got that? Everything in your life is part of His perfect plan for you.

First, you were created for a customized purpose by a loving God who knew you before you were born. Therefore, no matter where you might be at this moment, if you haven't yet found God's purpose for your life, you need to stop what you're doing and start looking.

Second, no matter how many good, bad, or ugly things have happened to you, God can still redirect your life to reflect His glory. And there is absolutely nothing in your past—or your present—that He can't use.

Third, even though it might be foggy outside, and even though you might be a little unclear about exactly where God wants you, that's okay. Maybe you veered off for a year, maybe even a decade or two. But that's all right. If nothing else, the story of Joseph should tell you that a certain amount of flailing around is perfectly normal. When we come into this world—kicking and screaming—very few of us know exactly what we're supposed to do when we grow up.

That's okay—start where you are, right now.

A SENSE OF HOPE

More than anything, as God puts you back on track, He wants to give you a sense of hope. Only God-given hope will sustain you as you move forward in life. To use a fancy word, God-given hope is what I'd call a *prerequisite,* meaning you're not going anywhere without it.

I have talked to any number of people who are living with a sense of hopelessness instead. "Am I ever going to get where I am supposed to be?" "Am I ever going to get it right?" "Is life ever going to work for me?" Most of these people have lost whatever hope they had. One little boy said, "Hope is wishing for something you know you are never going to get," and that's what a lot of folks feel.

To get a better idea of where hope comes from, let's take a look at another verse. God gave this verse to the prophet Jeremiah to encourage the Israelites as they went into captivity in Babylon many years after Joseph saved their nation back in Egypt. And I believe that this verse should encourage you as you move on in your own journey.

> "For I know the plans that I have for you," declares the LORD, "plans for welfare and not for calamity to give you a future and a hope." (Jeremiah 29:11)

Now, I can immediately hear some of you saying, "Hey, I'm glad somebody knows those plans, 'cause I sure don't!"

But listen to what the Lord is declaring: "And let Me tell you this," He says, "the plans I have for you are not for bad; they are for good! I will give you a future—a tomorrow—and a hope."

Have you ever seen people who have lost their hope? I certainly have. People lose their hope because they don't see a future. Yesterday was bleak…today is bleak…and tomorrow doesn't look any better. The weather report for your life says "No sunshine. One hundred percent chance of thunderstorms." There's nothing out there that has your number on it—nothing good, nothing dealing with purpose, calling, or destiny. It's dark, and the sun is nowhere to be found.

GREAT VERSE, NOT SO GREAT CHAPTER

But look at something else here. Jeremiah 29:11, which talks about God's *good* plan for the Israelites, is found in a sort of bad chapter. This is not a great verse in a great chapter; it's a great verse in a not so great chapter. So if you are having a bad life, this verse will fit right in!

Israel was in captivity in Babylon: "Thus says the LORD of hosts, the God of Israel, to all the exiles whom I have sent into exile from Jerusalem to Babylon" (v. 4). Verse 11 was written for people who had been placed in exile in judgment for rebelling against God. They were under the disciplining hand of God for their sins. They were being spanked, if you will. And to make it worse, the place where they were held captive was about as pagan as you can get. Babylon was not where the Christians hung out. This was a pagan pit—evil, idolatrous, and a terrible place to live, especially if you were an Israelite.

On top of all that, the Bible says that the Israelites' own preachers were leading them astray. They were giving other folks false hope in the name of God. "Come here; give your tithe; get rich. You're serving God. You're not going to get sick."

That's false prophecy. That's not true—never has been, never will be.

Of course God heals; of course God blesses. But to give people the impression that serving God means the end of all problems—well, that's just a lie. The Israelites were in a desperate situation, in negative circumstances, under divine discipline, in a pagan land. And to make things even worse, they were being led astray by the very people they should have been able to trust the most, the prophets.

Yet in the midst of this hopelessness and discouragement, along comes verse 11: If you're looking for hope, if you're tired of aimlessness, wandering, and meandering, this verse gives you the answer. Because God looks at us in our miserable state and says, "I still have a plan. It's not over. I still have a divine purpose for your life."

CAN I KNOW?

But how do you—in the here and now, at this precise moment, wherever you find yourself, standing or sitting or even walking around as you read these words—*how do you honestly know that God still has a plan for you?*

The answer is amazingly simple: You're still alive! God has a plan for every single person He ever created, a plan that never goes out of date. You've seen the milk at the supermarket, when it's been on the shelves a few days beyond the date it's supposed to come off. Well, you can be assured that God's plans don't have pull dates.

Even if you've missed God's plan entirely for years and years and years, that plan can still swing into operation the minute you're ready to step up and step in, with God at your side. Your plan might be somewhat modified from what it would have been twenty years ago, if you'd paid attention then, but that's no big deal. God can adapt to fit anything that ever comes up, in every life that will ever be lived.

So let's talk about "stepping up and stepping in," which I urge you to do in three separate moves.

1: Step up in faith.

Have you ever seen a blind man with a Seeing Eye dog? Now that's walking by faith. A person who is truly blind can't see the sidewalk in front of his feet. He can't tell the difference between a six-inch curb and a sixty-foot drop-off. He might know where he wants to go, but his own two eyes won't tell him when he gets there!

Nevertheless, that man believes in something. He believes that what his dog sees will be translated into some kind of reliable signal that will tell him whether to go, stop, turn right, or turn left. And he will pick up those signals by staying connected with the dog.

It's a faith walk. If a blind person had to depend entirely on his own eyes, he couldn't tell the difference between a tree full of leaves and a tray full of loaves.

So why does he trust a dog?

Because that dog has something he doesn't have.

And it's the same with you and God. I know it might look dark right now. I know it might be unclear exactly where God is taking you. It might even be pitch black outside, so murky you can't see your hand in front of your face.

Why does He make you stop at the corner so long? Maybe there's some traffic coming your way. Why does He seem to keep you stuck, delayed, hindered? I don't know why, but I know what He said. God has the eyes of eternity that you and I don't have. "'I know the plans I have for you.' I know you don't know all the details. I know it's not fully fleshed out, and I know that things can sometimes come at you so fast you want to duck."

But God still says, "I have a plan, and I know how it works." And better still, "My plans are for your welfare and not for calamity." He says that His plans involve a future, they involve your tomorrow, and they contain hope for you.

God has your tomorrow covered even though you haven't been there yet. God works outside of time, so He's not held back by the limitations you and I labor with. He has already scoped out tomorrow. And He has come back to tell you that He has the plan scoped out too.

"I know it's dark, but don't walk off. I have a future for you," He says.

That's why, just like the blind man and his Seeing Eye dog, you need to hold on and stay connected. Have faith. That way when God moves, you'll know it.

Let me give you just one more example before we move to the second step. Quite often I fly from Dallas to various cities around the country. During these trips a number of factors have to come together:

1. I have to identify a flight schedule that will take me to my intended destination.
2. That plane has to operate on a timetable that tells me when it's leaving and when it's arriving, and the pilot has to have a route all worked out in advance.
3. The airline has to set a price that I can afford to pay.

Once I've found a flight with the combination of these three factors, the airline puts my name in a computer, and everything is ready to go. Now let me explain what I'm *not* going to do when I arrive at the airport.

- I am not going to ask them to explain how the plane works. I am not going to ask them what buttons they plan to push and what the equipment will do when they push each button.

- I am also not going to check on the route they plan to take. I don't care whether they go this way or that way, and I am not going to debate with them about how many feet up or down they fly that plane before they turn on the cruise control.
- And I am not going to argue about the price after I've already made my reservation and paid my money.

Contrary to all these things I *could* do, I am simply going to assume that the airline I am taking has hired personnel with all of the knowledge and experience they need so I can just find my seat and chill out until I get where I'm going.

If the plane goes *boop!* during the flight, that won't bother me, because I will have boarded that airplane with certain basic assumptions. I will trust them to know how to do what they promised they'd do, to get me safely where they promised to take me.

How much more should we trust God when He makes promises about where He wants to take us?

2: *Step away from your mistakes.*

The stories of Paul, Peter, and Joseph should tell you all you need to know about making mistakes, as far as God and His purposes for you are concerned. The lives of all those men were filled with mistakes of one kind or another—with bad things and ugly things.

But God was able to take every single one and turn it around for good.

When my wife and I were first married, back when our kids were little and I was still in school, we watched our pennies just like many of you are doing right now. In fact, watching pennies is something we've never quite gotten away from.

One way we did that was to be careful with our food budget. That meant we sometimes saw the same dish more than once, although due to my wife's incredible talent in the kitchen, it didn't always have the same face. It might show up as mashed potatoes and peas on Monday and shepherd's pie on Thursday.

On the other hand, it might come back a day or two later as something no one except my wife herself could ever recognize. She'd chop it, dice it, mix in some cheese, splash some cream of mushroom soup over the top, dress it up with some parsley, put it on a fancy tray, give it a French-sounding name, and we thought we had something brand-new!

These meals came from the hand of a master, but what we actually had was leftovers. And if you insisted on seeing it as the dregs of another day, you'd condemn yourself to a meal without pleasure, a meal without promise or adventure, a meal without hope that there could ever be anything better than what you'd already known.

But if you saw what our master chef created as a brand-new gourmet treat, you'd have an entirely different experience.

God sometimes works the same way in your life. If you bring Him what you have left over, whether it's good, bad, or ugly, He can dice it, chop it, put cream of Holy Ghost soup over the top, and turn it into something you never would have thought possible.

You just need to step away, turn it over to Him, and let Him do His thing. In the same way, I didn't hover when my wife was reinventing my dinner. I knew everything would come out a lot better if I kept my hands off.

I'm not asking you to keep your hands entirely off your own life, but I am asking you to step back far enough to let God work without hindrance. And just like the blind man we mentioned above, you'll know exactly when to start moving again.

3: *Step into God's promise.*

When God told the Israelites in Jeremiah 29 that He had a plan for them, He gave them hope. But hope doesn't do much good in a vacuum. It needs a nurturing environment. He didn't give them permission to take that hope and then just sit back and do nothing.

On the contrary, He told them exactly what He wanted them to do in the meantime while He was working out some of the details for their future.

> "Build houses and live in them; and plant gardens and eat their produce. Take wives and become the fathers of sons and daughters, and take wives for your sons and give your daughters to husbands, that they may bear sons and daughters; and multiply there and do not decrease. Seek the welfare of the city where I have sent you into exile, and pray to the LORD on its behalf; for in its welfare you will have welfare." (vv. 5–7)

In other words, get on with your lives!

You need to do the same. While you're waiting on God to turn things around, seize the moment. He might not do everything in a single day, so build houses and live in them. Plant gardens and eat what you grow; become as productive as you possibly can. Don't sit and do nothing. Do all that's at your hand to do—maximize your potential.

A lot of us, while we wait for God, think we can do nothing when there is plenty to do.

Go way back to the very beginning of the book. "Maximizing your potential" is exactly what we were talking about when we mentioned education, training, and building a résumé.

The apostle Paul went to school as a young man and maximized his potential. He didn't become a scholar by accident. Peter maximized his potential in an entirely different way, by learning from his failure. And Joseph maximized his potential over and over again, by trusting God and allowing Him to turn every ugly thing that happened to him into something good.

God did all the behind-the-scenes work by bringing everything—and every person—together at just the right moment, but Joseph had to prepare himself as he went along. He had to learn how to oversee his boss's household, how to listen for the Lord's voice, and how to manage the economy of an entire country.

Most important, Paul, Peter, and Joseph all had to learn how to trust the Lord, how *to work within His plan for their lives to accomplish what He had in mind for them.* And ultimately, while they waited on Him they learned an awful lot by doing the very things the Lord told the Israelites to do.

BECOME A BLESSING FIRST

Seek the welfare of others. Find out how you can be a blessing. Pray for the city you live in right now and its people, for its welfare is your welfare.

This is one of the fundamental keys. As you *become a blessing,* you set yourself up to *be blessed.* One of the reasons we lose hope is that we become concerned about one person only…and guess who that one person often is.

If you have messed up and the only person you see is you, then you are helping to do yourself in. But God tells us to seek the welfare of others and become a blessing. He says, "While you're waiting on Me to do something for you, do something good for others."

That's what Paul meant when he quoted Jesus, saying, "'It is more blessed to give than to receive'" (Acts 20:35). Because by blessing others, you literally open up a channel for God to come through when He blesses you.

That's what God refers to a little later in Jeremiah 29 when He says:

> "Then you will call upon Me and come and pray to Me, and I will listen to you. You will seek Me and find Me when you search for Me with all your heart. I will be found by you," declares the LORD, "and I will restore your fortunes and will gather you from all the nations and from all the places where I have driven you," declares the LORD, "and I will bring you back to the place from where I sent you into exile." (vv. 12–14)

Unfortunately, most of us don't read verse 13 as it's written. Instead, we read it, "When you seek the solution, you'll find the solution." But that's not what it says. It says, "You will seek *Me* and find *Me* when you search for *Me* with all your heart."

That's the ultimate answer for all of us. Paul confirms this in Romans 8:28:

And we know that God causes all things to work together for good to those who love God, to those who are called according to His purpose.

God says, "I have the plans. Don't go looking for the plans; look for Me. I know where I put them. You find Me, you'll find the plans. You want to know your calling, find Me. I know it. You want to find your mate, find Me first. I know where he or she is."

In Christ "are hidden all the treasures of wisdom and knowledge" (Colossians 2:3). How can we possibly look anywhere else?

WHAT GOD INITIATES, GOD COMPLETES

Finally, I know that many of you wish you could turn back the hands of time and live parts of your lives all over again. I know that you feel like you've been in the game too long and you don't know how much longer it's going to take to pull something meaningful out of your life.

But still, despite all your questions, God has a plan for you. He knows what it is, He guarantees that it's a good one, and He offers you a future and a hope. God is inviting you to participate with Him in the drama of the ages.

- You don't know which way to go…seek Him.
- You are in pain…seek Him.
- You are confused…seek Him.
- You are tired of waiting…seek Him.

If you come to Dallas and ask me what to do with your life, I am going to send you right back home and right back to Him. Because God has not told me His plan for you. He's the only One who knows! What God initiates, God completes. But you say, "I'm in a mess. It's the biggest mess anyone ever made. You don't know my mess!"

There's only one answer for that.

You don't know my God.

Multnomah Publishers®

The publisher and author would love to hear your comments about this book. *Please contact us at:*
www.lifechangebooks.com

In Closing...

If you don't have a personal relationship with God that fills your heart with hope no matter what your circumstances might be, I urge you to turn to Him right now. Wherever you are, whatever you're doing, focus your heart and mind on Jesus Christ and pray this simple prayer:

Dear Lord Jesus, I believe that You are the Son of God and the only way to God. I believe that You died on the cross for my sins and rose again so that I might be forgiven and receive eternal life. I confess my sinfulness before You and hold nothing back. I repent of my sins, I accept Your sacrifice on my behalf, and I turn to You for mercy and forgiveness and the gift of eternal life.

I also ask You to take charge of my new life and direct it toward tomorrow. I ask You to bring hope back into my life, knowing that You have a unique plan for me. I ask You to guide my footsteps from this day forward.

Thank You! Amen.

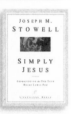
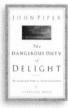

The Urban Alternative